Extreme Machines
ON ICE AND SNOW

PATRICIA ARMENTROUT

The Rourke Press, Inc.
Vero Beach, Florida 32964

Patricia Armentrout specializes in nonfiction writing and has had several book series published for primary schools. She resides in Cincinnati with her husband and two children.

PHOTO CREDITS:
© Armentrout: pages 18, 19; © Norris Clark/Intl. Stock: page 15; © Corel Corporation: page 13; © Defense Visual Information Center: page 12; © Tom & Michele Grimm/Intl. Stock: page 4; © Kim Karpeles: page 16; © Randy Green: page 21; © Jeff Osborne: cover, page 9; © Oshkosh Truck Corporation of Oshkosh, Wisconsin: pages 7, 10; © Panther Airboat: page 22; © Schmidt Engineering & Equipment, Inc.: page 6

EDITORIAL SERVICES:
Penworthy Learning Systems

Library of Congress Cataloging-in-Publication Data

Armentrout, Patricia, 1960-
    Extreme machines on ice and snow / Patricia Armentrout.
      p. cm. — (Extreme machines)
    Includes index.
    Summary: Describes special machines such as snowmobiles, snow plows, ice breakers, and tundra buggies which are used to remove or travel on ice and snow.
    ISBN 1-57103-210-X
    1. Snowmobiles—Juvenile literature. 2. Snow plows—Juvenile literature.
[1. Snowmobiles. 2. Snow plows.] I. Armentrout, Patricia. 1960- II. Title
III. Series: Extreme machines.
TL234.2.A76 1998
629.225—dc21
                                      98–24064
                                           CIP
                                         AC

Printed in the USA

TABLE OF CONTENTS

EXTREME MACHINES FOR EXTREME WEATHER

People use machines every day of the year. Special machines are used in **extreme** (ik STREEM) weather, such as ice and snow. Machines make our work easier and can make play more fun.

Some machines are used to remove ice and snow. Some machines are used to travel on ice and snow.

Ski lift machines use strong cables to move heavy gondolas and skiers across snowy mountains.

CLEARING THE ROADS

A snowstorm can bring several feet of snow at one time. Too much snow on roads can make travel difficult. When streets are snow covered, highway crews get out the snow plows.

Rotary plows blow snow away from the road.

Plows are angled to push the snow to one side.

Plows are used to clear snow from roadways. A plow is a blade attached to a powerful truck or tractor. A single-blade plow pushes snow to one side. A V-shaped plow on the front of a tractor or truck will clear the snow on both sides at the same time.

CLEARING THE TRACKS

Snow and ice-covered railroad tracks can be dangerous. An engine, called a **locomotive** (LO kuh MO tiv), is used to clear the tracks. Some locomotives use a V-shaped blade attached to the front. As the engine moves along the tracks the plow pushes the snow to the sides.

In mountain areas, where snow can be very deep, a locomotive with a big **rotary** (RO tuh ree) snowplow is used to clear the tracks. The engine moves along the tracks as the big blade spins. A rotary snowplow can cut through deep snow drifts over 20 feet (6.1 meters) high.

Train tracks are cleared with plows attached to powerful locomotives.

CLEARING THE RUNWAYS

Airport runways are big and need special snow removal machines. Plow blades may not be enough to get the job done.

A big machine called a rotary snowblower is driven over piles of snow. The cutting action of the blades break up the snow, and the blower shoots the snow out of the way.

Ice can be more dangerous than snow. When temperatures fall below freezing, big tank trucks spray a special liquid on the runways to melt ice and snow.

Huge rotary snowblowers are used to clear airport runways.

CLEARING THE WATERWAYS

Temperatures below the freezing point can cause waterways to freeze. Snow and ice often block ports and shipping lanes. Ships cannot haul their cargo to other ports without clear waterways.

Polar Star is the first Coast Guard icebreaker to travel around Antarctica.

An icebreaker clears a path through frozen waters.

A special ship, called an icebreaker, is used to clear shipping lanes. An icebreaker is heavy and has a strong **hull** (HUL). An icebreaker rides up on the ice, crushing it and moving it out of the way. Cargo ships are able to get through by following the icebreaker's path.

FUN ON THE SNOW

Snow machines are not only for snow removal. Snowmobiles are machines built for fun on the snow.

Snowmobiles have an engine in the rear and two skis to support the front. The driver mounts the machine, like a motorcycle, and steers the skis with handlebars.

Snowmobile riders cruise at speeds up to 50 miles (80.5 kilometers) an hour through snow-covered fields and trails. Snowmobile clubs host racing events. Racing snowmobiles have powerful engines that allow the driver to go as fast as 120 miles (193.2 kilometers) an hour.

Snowmobile riding is a great way to enjoy the winter weather.

ICE RESURFACER

Ice rink operators all over the world use a unique machine, called an ice resurfacer, to scrape and smooth the surface of the ice. Ice skaters and hockey players need a clean, smooth surface to skate on.

How does an ice resurfacer work? As the big machine is driven across the ice, it scrapes and collects ice shavings from the surface. At the same time, the machine washes and smooths the ice. The dirty water is vacuumed and stored inside a tank.

Finally the ice resurfacer spreads a thin layer of hot water on the ice. As the hot water freezes, it leaves the ice in perfect condition for skating.

An ice resurfacer can prepare a fresh ice skating surface in about ten minutes.

SNOW GROOMER

A snow groomer is a big tractor with treads, not wheels. Snow groomers are used at many ski resorts and in other snowy areas.

A snow groomer prepares, or "grooms," the slopes for skiers. Groomers have attachments in the front and rear. The attachments break up ice-covered snow and pack down fresh snow.

Wide crawler treads keep snow groomers on the slope.

A snow groomer has front and rear attachments that pack and groom the snow.

Groomers also carry passengers. Skiers can board the huge tractor for a ride to the back country. The back country offers skiers fresh powdery snow instead of the packed snow found on groomed slopes.

TUNDRA VEHICLE

A special vehicle called a **tundra** (TUN druh) buggy is a popular touring vehicle in the Arctic regions of Canada. People ride in safety and comfort while viewing polar bears and other wildlife. Photographers take tundra buggy tours because they can get close to polar bears without putting themselves in danger.

The tundra buggy sets high on six-foot tires. The passenger compartment looks like a bus with many windows on both sides. Inside the buggy is enough room to seat 12 people.

Six-foot tires on this tundra buggy keep polar bears at a safe distance.

GLOSSARY

extreme (ik STREEM) — beyond normal limits, as in extremely cold or extremely powerful

hull (HUL) — the body of a ship

locomotive (LO kuh MO tiv) — a car used to move railroad cars; an engine

maneuver (muh NOO ver) — a skillful movement

rotary (RO tuh ree) — turning on an axis like a wheel; having a spinning part

tundra (TUN druh) — treeless plains of the northern Arctic regions

The bottom of an ice airboat is built tough to withstand the extreme conditions of ice and snow.

INDEX

FURTHER READING

Find out more about Extreme Machines with this helpful book:
Marston, Hope Irvin. *Snowplows*. Dodd, Mead & Company, 1986.

ELEMENTARY SCHOOL